Essential Elegance

Essential Elegance

THE INTERIORS OF SOLÍS BETANCOURT

José Solís Betancourt and Paul Sherrill
Written by Dana Demange
Principal Photography by Marcos Galvany

THE MONACELLI PRESS

In memory of Jorge Colón-Nevares, a dear friend, mentor,
patron, and an inspiration in so many ways. Jorge was the epitome of
a true gentleman. We miss him dearly.

Contents

Introduction

The Solís Betancourt style resists definition. Their look is all about tactile luxury, yet it is a luxury that is always understated and refined. Their style embraces color, but the subdued palettes they build and layer within every interior do not alone distinguish the space. Their rooms contain careful arrangements of finely crafted antiques, yet the addition of modern elements contributes to a timeless aesthetic experience. In sum, the Solís Betancourt philosophy is about context: their design is meaningful because it relies on the full participation of the client, a complete understanding of how a family will live in and enjoy a given space, and an attention to detail that transforms the home into an ever-evolving reflection of the owner's life.

For Solís Betancourt, this understanding of context always begins with an appreciation for the interior architecture of a house. José Solís's architectural training becomes apparent in the meticulous treatment of elevations and a highly developed sense of proportion and symmetry. Spatial relationships of scale and axial vistas are carefully considered, as are the visual and practical implications of every detail. "The basic truth is that beautiful architecture really does not require much decorating," says Solís.

Naturally, the architectural requirements for each project vary. Paul Sherrill and Solís have designed houses from the ground up, and they have assisted clients in identifying property to purchase before guiding them through a renovation process. In considering interiors, they might embellish a plain space with cased openings, crown moldings, and wainscoting to create a period feel, or, conversely, they might play a reductive role, stripping interiors to minimal, contemporary settings. In such a space, the strategic placement of an important piece of furniture—a Baroque console or Regency armoire, for example—can serve an architectural function.

A sense of place has a profound effect on the way Solís Betancourt envisions a project. The majority of their houses are located along the East Coast and in the Caribbean. For Solís, who grew up in Puerto Rico, the island vernacular comes naturally. In several projects, he has translated this aesthetic into the epitome of tropical elegance, comfortable and full of sensuality. Many of the firm's residences are in the Washington, D. C., area. "I think that the Chesapeake and Potomac region has gone unnoticed as a place for great design because of Washington's role as the seat of government and power," says Sherrill. "However, there is a relaxed style in the area that is an amalgam of our nation's own diverse styles, mixed in with a dose of Southern influence." A North Carolina native, Sherrill is fully conversant with the gracious sophistication and hospitable spirit of Southern homes.

But the sense of place that inspires design need not be so literal. Many clients who describe their vision express a love for a far-off destination. The countryside of Normandy can become the inspirational motif, or the pearly light of Delft, as depicted in an interior by Vermeer. Sherrill and Solís invite their clients to bring images of rooms and furnishings that they like as well as images they dislike. This exercise helps the clients consolidate their own ideas into a vision, which the designers then translate and organize into a tangible framework. During subsequent client meetings, Sherrill and Solís present a design proposal filled with elaborate drawings that show the interior architecture, proposed furniture arrangements, and window and floor treatments. Samples of the materials and finishes also help illustrate the plan being suggested.

Sherrill and Solís value the collaborative process that takes place among the design experts and artisans on a project. The close alliance between interior decorator, architect, and landscape designer helps to generate a common vision in which every detail fits together in a comprehensive and seamless manner. The drawings eventually become instructional documents for communication with an extensive network of craftspeople. This group of professionals includes drapery and upholstery workshops, weavers, cabinetmakers, masons, and muralists, decorative painters, metal workers, and glass blowers. The designers also work with the clients to commission site-specific works from renowned artists.

Using their extensive technical knowledge, Sherrill and Solís have devised ingenious solutions for integrating mechanical, lighting, and entertainment systems. If an appropriate solution does not exist in the marketplace, they devise a product and have it custom-made. This innovative spirit has led Solís Betancourt to design a signature lighting collection. This line of sconces, lanterns, and table lamps is a sleek, pared-down reinterpretation of traditional fixtures.

For Solís Betancourt, filling interiors with furnishings, textiles, and art has a somewhat contradictory effect: a series of very deliberate and calculated choices contribute to a look that appears effortless, as though the collection of objects came together little by little over decades. Their goal is to achieve a balanced look between formal and informal, traditional and contemporary, while always keeping comfort and livability in mind. There is a striking simplicity to their arrangement of furniture and art: the look is controlled, never excessive, yet they are not afraid to bring in dramatic elements to surprise and enchant the eye. A dazzling mirrored mosaic wall might illuminate a white marble vestibule, or a finely carved terra-cotta torso placed inside an upholstered niche might act as the focal point of a formal dining room. Often, the client asks them to act as visual editors, making choices about which objects in their art or antiques collection should be kept or stored and which need to be updated or replaced. Clients may travel with Sherrill and Solís on buying trips to help build a new collection of furniture, art, and other treasures.

For Sherrill, who grew up in a family of artisans and studied art as well as interior design, the soul of a home comes from its display of paintings, sculptures, and other decorative objects that are meaningful to the owner. "I have a deep respect for any handcrafted object that was made with talent and passion," says Sherrill. "Such pieces are not only important aesthetically, but also take on a spiritual quality."

Most notably in a Solís Betancourt room, comfort centers around the sensuous fabrics that might envelop a spacious armchair, cushion a delicate settee, or softly frame a set of French doors. Fabric might be used as an accent, lining niches or bookcases as an enriched background for the objects on display. Or fabric might take on a more important role, covering the ceiling and walls to create a tactile and alluring environment. Nubby linens, shimmering silks, regal damasks, are subtly layered into a serene composition that begs to be touched and enjoyed. The use of color enhances this inviting experience. "The days of spartan white interiors have passed," says Solís. "Today, we find clients craving color and pattern." Solís Betancourt tends to favor pigmented plaster walls, which lend warmth and texture to a room as does the selection of artwork.

Perhaps the Solís Betancourt style is hard to define because it is linked less to a set look than to an emotional experience. These are interiors that offer a moment of transcendence, a glimpse beyond everyday routine. These are rooms to come home to, sanctuaries that offer a sense of protection, tranquility, and beauty.

A Neutral Palette

Tucked amid the foliage of Washington's Rock Creek Park, this house combines old-world charm with the best of modern city living. Once a cinder-block eyesore on a block filled with stately mansions, the modest cottage has been transformed into a classical pavilion that takes full advantage of beautiful parkland views. For the interiors, Sherrill and Solís envisioned a refined combination of traditional and contemporary elements.

The residence may seem tiny from its delicate facade, but a grand staircase in the entry foyer immediately prepares guests to rethink their initial expectations. Configuring a gracious floor plan required gutting the interiors and replacing a central chimneystack in the entry with a skylit opening that illuminates the waterfall staircase below. Its iron balustrade guides visitors downstairs to the public rooms on the lower level where stained wood windows and French doors frame the majestic forest views. The overall color scheme of the house is a blend of muted creams and taupes punctuated with hints of steely blue and amethyst. A masterful layering of textures and materials enriches this tonally even palette. Rough-hewn beams give the rooms an aged and historic feel that is balanced by the crisp lines of the coffered ceilings.

In the living room, linen draperies divide the grand space into more intimate seating areas. The clean lines of the cocoa-colored mohair sofa and linen upholstered club chairs complement the client's collection of French and Asian antiques. In another corner, a chaise is adorned with velvet and chenille damask pillows and a channel-quilted silk throw. Chunky sea-grass carpets and a patterned Chinese rug break up the expanse of the stone and gray-washed wooden floors.

A massive concrete fireplace was added to give solidity to the airy room.

The dining room is a few steps higher than the living room and can be closed off using pocket doors with seeded glass panes. This elevation serves as the perfect stage for informal speakers and performers addressing guests gathered in the living room below. A sleek marble dining table, crowned by a sculptural butcher's rack, is surrounded by modern yet comfortable upholstered armchairs.

The adjoining breakfast room and kitchen are also defined by the juxtaposition of old and new elements. A pristine glass top sits on a patinated art deco bistro table while Moroccan tiles, rough-hewn beams, and stainless-steel shelves and appliances evoke tradition, with a twist. Off the kitchen, a shaded courtyard is the perfect spot for summer dining al fresco.

The main entrance level houses a grand master suite and guest rooms. In the master bedroom, the geometric lines of the iron poster bed and checkerboard hemp carpet echo the grid of the French doors and coffered ceiling while sensuous ceramic lamps and plush eggplant velvet pillows offer a softer element. The bedroom can be closed off from the sunny views with remote-controlled suede draperies. The sitting area feels like a magical porch floating amid the forest canopy.

ABOVE: Anthony Barnes and Solís Betancourt collaborated to transform a mundane elevation into a charming cottage facade. OPPOSITE: Weathered shutters add privacy and charm to the entrance.

Draperies in the living area soften the room without
obscuring the parkland views.

In the living room, the curves of the furniture contrast with the tall, rectilinear windows and coffered ceiling.

The living room windows were left exposed to accentuate the link to the outdoors.
OVERLEAF: A lantern designed by Solís Betancourt hangs above a porch-like area in the master bedroom.

ABOVE: A film-strip painting by Los Angeles–based artist Carter Potter hangs in the dining room.
OPPOSITE: In the kitchen, functional stainless steel is paired with the textured finishes of
terra-cotta tiles and rustic beams.

In the entrance hall, a suede and nailhead upholstered mirror hangs above a French console.

A trellis covered in willow branches provides shelter from the sun and privacy in the outdoor courtyard.

Lyrical Dreamscape

The owners of this neo-colonial house in Potomac, Maryland, asked Solís Betancourt to rework the interiors as a chic but family-friendly environment. They requested a palette of muted grays, lavenders, and greens. Overall, the project included simplifying elaborate interior elevations and redesigning the finishes of the rooms.

In the entry hall, a heavy wood balustrade was replaced with a dainty iron railing, and the circular opening to the level below was closed off to give unobstructed access to the adjoining garden room. A marble table, Louis XVI chair, and flowing damask draperies are a prelude to the graceful interiors throughout the house.

The soft palette in the living room could very well have stemmed from the bouquets of flowers carved into the stone fireplace surround. An assortment of textured fabrics in silvery blues and shimmering mauves gives the room a quiet luxury. The gilt mirror and brackets are a regal touch that allows for the flair of seasonal floral arrangements. A landscape above the sofa, strikingly framed in gold, depicts a tranquil view of the Potomac River.

The painted furniture and sparkling chandelier give the dining room an airy lightness. The walls are covered with layers of tea paper that were hand painted and sanded to give a lightly distressed finish. On the main wall, there is a delicate mural of a spring garden filled with colorful birds. Curtains of strié printed silk trimmed with jade beads are used in both the dining room and living room, bringing a visual continuity to the two public spaces. Sherrill and Solís converted an arched niche with glass shelving into a rectangular mohair-lined alcove that dramatically sets off a terra-

Damask draperies in the entry frame the doorway to the central garden room.

cotta bust. A china closet was added to balance the doorway leading to the kitchen.

In the garden room, an Aubusson tapestry, small stone sculptures, framed prints, and wrought-iron side tables all evoke an aviary setting. The coffered ceiling was faux-painted to complement the bleached wood floors throughout most of the house. A set of French doors leads to a screened porch. This is one of several rooms intended for everyday family gatherings. In the adjoining breakfast room, a farm table and set of Swedish balloon-backed chairs offer an informal atmosphere. The stone wall of the hearth room receives a cheerful splash of raspberry red from the floral pillows, ceramic lamps, and draperies.

Upstairs, a tranquil blue predominates in the master bedroom. The rice paper wall covering, a carved Indian jali-style table, and settee with griffin armrests give the room a suggestion of the exotic.

Wrought-iron stair railings gracefully spiral up three floors.

The muted palette of the living room creates a serene atmosphere for entertaining. Hints of mauve and lavender are repeated throughout the rest of the house.

For the dining room, Sherrill and Solís chose a hand-painted wall covering
of flowering trees and exotic birds.

The leaf and twig chandelier above the breakfast room table continues the romantic
reference to nature, which is also repeated in the adjoining garden room.

Exotic birds are a
theme of the garden
room, seen in the
set of six prints, the
Aubusson tapestry,
and the fabrics.

36

The seating area in the master bedroom includes a carved Swedish settee and a stone jali-style table.

Old World Elegance

Entering this sumptuous 1930s Tudor-style residence is a passage into another realm, one that leaves the vicissitudes of modern-day living far behind. This sanctuary pays tribute to the owners' love of reading and learning, a passion that has guided them in building a collection of art, books, and antiquities.

Solís Betancourt collaborated with the owners on every aspect of the project. They helped to identify a suitable property to house their clients' treasures and accompanied them on trips to England and France to acquire furnishings that would complement the collection. Overall, the task was to respectfully transform the house into an environment that would enhance the collection without making the space feel like a museum.

The entry foyer introduces architectural elements that are original to the house—Gothic-style paneled doors, terra-cotta tiles, leaded glass windows, and rough-hewn oak beams. A pair of English consoles, refinished in a neutral wash, display ancient Egyptian Canopic jars, an early Greek terra-cotta head, and a series of Renaissance drawings.

Steps lead down to a regal drawing room, where a second-century marble statue of Artemis keeps her steady gaze on the surroundings. The billowing folds of her tunic seem as real as the celadon draperies and silk sheers flowing behind her. The Aubusson carpet, damask upholsteries, and Medici tapestry add tactile richness to the space. The room was planned around an antique harpsichord and a piano, instruments that the owners both play. Two Palladian-style bookcases, one early nineteenth century and the other a faithful reproduction, flank a doorway in the back of the room.

Solís designed a special low-voltage lighting system to illuminate the art without damaging it. The lights are wired from the ceiling and activate when hung from the

The entrance hall introduces the aesthetic of the house: a Tudor-style setting for a rich collection of art and antiques.

supporting bronze picture rail, an ingenious system that leaves a pristine wall if a work is removed for a museum exhibition.

In the dining room, a massive Regency table invites guests to gather around and settle into one of the stately chairs, adorned with églomisé splats with a coat of arms. A group of Dürer engravings and a Flemish master's depiction of Mary Magdalene are hung in front of a silk panel. Across the room, a sixteenth-century triptych sits on a sideboard amid a casual assortment of ancient Greek vessels.

The library is the metaphorical heart of the house. The fireplace wall was built out to accommodate new bookshelves and a sound system; the new millwork is a seamless match with the original. The heavy velvet draperies, which extend to cover the shelves, were designed to protect the books from light and dust. They are reversible, one side bark colored for summer months, the other a deep chocolate for winter.

Private rooms are on a more intimate scale. The breakfast room contains a fine collection of Greek ceramics protected by specially designed stands. Café curtains provide privacy without hiding the dramatic French doors. The doorway to the study is on axis with a favorite painting, a jewel-toned Adoration scene. This work guided the choice of colors and textures in the room. The eggplant velvet that lines the niches was inspired by the Virgin's cloak, the faded green of the cabinets matches the entablature frame. The small Knole-style sofa provides a perfect vantage point to view the collection of Roman figurines.

Upstairs, the master bedroom suite is a study in ethereal lightness. The craftsmanship of the Adam-style plasterwork and cabinetry in the bathroom is exquisite. Three shades of lavender add a sense of height to the recessed ceiling panels. In the bedroom, an embroidered Chinese silk hanging, lined with plum sateen wool, establishes the color scheme. Solís Betancourt designed the gilded iron bed, crowned with armillary spheres personalized to reflect the owners' astrological signs. The dainty Louis XVI side table and settee complement the room's soft and romantic style.

A typically eclectic grouping: Egyptian Canopic jars set on an English console with a Renaissance portrait above.

The main drawing room houses an elegant collection of fine period furniture, musical instruments, and works of art. On the right, a Roman statue of Artemis is placed on axis with the fireplace.

44

ABOVE: An assortment of fine textiles adorns a Georgian sofa.
OPPOSITE: In one corner of the drawing room, a Regency chair and George I settee
are gathered around a nineteenth-century English games table.

ABOVE: In the stair hall, a Renaissance painting celebrating the triumph of a Roman emperor hangs above a collection of Greek rhyton ceramics. OPPOSITE: Works by Albrecht Dürer surround a sixteenth-century depiction of Mary Magdalene by the Master of the Parrot.

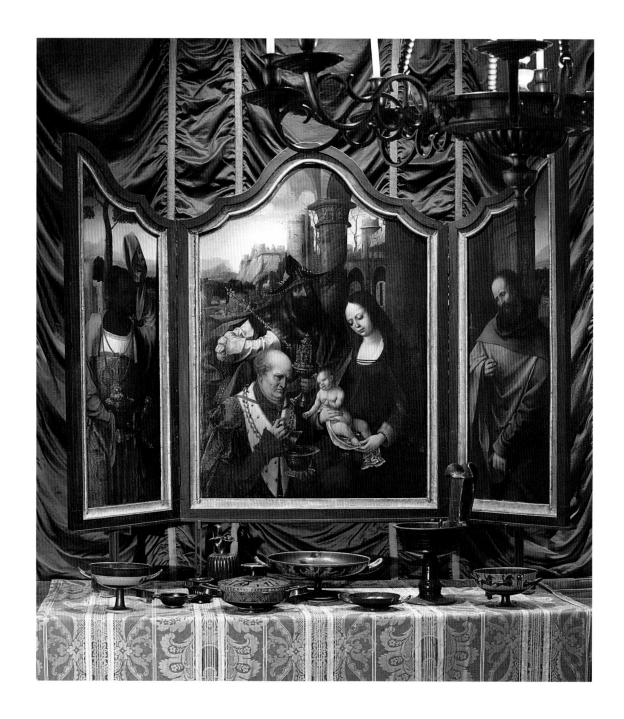

ABOVE: An early-sixteenth-century triptych of the Adoration of the Magi rests on the dining room sideboard. OPPOSITE: In the breakfast room, Regency chairs surround a Biedermeier table. Sherrill and Solís added the walnut coffered ceiling and cabinetry, which houses art books and Attic terra-cotta vases.

In the art-filled library
a reversible throw
on the sofa keeps the
room pet-friendly.

In the study, a marble portrait bust of Marcus Aurelius sits on axis with the drawing room. Niches provide a display for a fine collection of Greek and Roman glass and bronze pieces.

ABOVE: Ancient glass housed in one of the study's niches. OPPOSITE: A sofa offers a comfortable vantage point to study the collections or to play chess on the George III penwork games table.

ABOVE: The custom-designed master bed incorporates armillary sphere finials that reflect the owners' astrological signs. OPPOSITE: In the bathroom, modern conveniences are concealed within the Adam-style plasterwork.

Romanticism Reborn

Reminiscent of the French chateaux of Normandy, this residence in Potomac, Maryland, evokes the enchantment and timelessness of a fairy tale. The interiors were inspired by the traditional architecture, but they also contain modern references that provide an overall look of freshness and simplicity. Solís Betancourt envisioned spaces filled with sunlight and graceful furnishings conducive to elegant entertaining while comfortable and relaxed for family life.

The turreted entry room introduces a romantic spirit. Butter-colored rolled plaster walls and ivy-filled pots lend an inviting warmth to the stone floors and stairs of the spare stair hall. An eighteenth-century Aubusson tapestry brings color to the room while also making a historical and stylistic reference. The wrought-iron sconces, railing, and door handles are a consistent architectural detail throughout the house.

The dining room combines sophistication with an easy luxury. A carefully orchestrated interplay of texture and pattern enriches the setting. Antiqued celadon velvet softens two niches that flank the entrance. Across the room this fabric is repeated in the flowing draperies that frame a series of French doors. A modern interpretation of tapestry upholstery, printed velvet with distressed gilt touches, covers the Louis XIII-style chairs. Damask-lined walls create a subdued atmosphere, enlivened by the sparkle of reflective light from the hand-carved mirror, crystal chandelier, and sconces.

The delicate pistachio, lilac, and peach accents in the adjoining living room could have sprung from a shimmering Impressionist painting. Floral motifs on the Chinese folding screen and in the paintings are echoed in the silk embroidered draperies. A limestone fireplace dominates the room architecturally while an assortment of glass and ivory-colored tables lends a modern sensibility. Chunky sisal carpeting keeps the

Architect Anthony Barnes developed the Normandy-style structure that inspired Solís Betancourt's earthy palette found throughout the interior.

room casual as does the aged finish of the fumed Russian white oak flooring used throughout the house.

The spacious kitchen is central to family life. Antiqued strié painted cabinets with stained cane inserts give a rustic feel to the area as does the v-grooved plank wood ceiling with its light paint wash. In warm weather, meals can be served outdoors on the nearby shaded loggia or by the pool in front of the guesthouse.

In the library, the oak paneling, pilasters, and ceiling beams were heavily distressed and rubbed with celadon-colored paint. This pale green subtly reappears in the upholstery fabrics, with tapestry pillows to bring color and pattern to the space. The shelves are lined with a finely woven rust-colored grass cloth to complement a collection of terracotta antiquities, bronze sculptures, and leatherbound books. The chandelier and gilded lamps beside the sofa add a dash of contemporary flair.

ABOVE: The door into the turreted entry stair hall is embellished with ironwork and strap hinges.
OPPOSITE AND OVERLEAF: A painting by French artist
Jules Pascin echoes the soft colors of the main living room.

In the dining room, a
pair of velvet-lined
niches contain
Guatemalan colonial-
style mirrors
surrounded by a set
of Ashworth Brothers
plates.

66

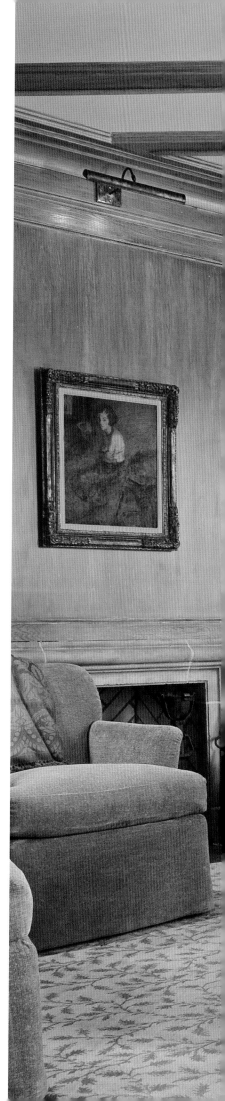

In the library, oak cabinetry was heavily distressed and paint-rubbed to provide an aged patina. Comfortable armchairs are on casters so they can be easily pulled up to the central oak table.
OVERLEAF: The guesthouse faces the rear elevation across the pool.

ABOVE: A painting by Alan Feltus hangs above a seating group upholstered in silk and linen in the master bedroom. OPPOSITE: A Chinese deco-style plaster sconce table is framed by damask draperies.

ABOVE: Cascading embroidered bed draperies are tempered by a
tailored counterpane. OPPOSITE: Framed specimens of pressed coral
flank a window in the master bedroom.

Urban Tapestry

Paul Sherrill's jewel box apartment in downtown Washington is a stylish ode to city living. Located in a historic building, the residence boasts high ceilings, casement windows, and two working fireplaces. The space is small but richly appointed with ample room for gracious living and entertaining. Sherrill was inspired by his love of sixteenth-century Dutch paintings of interiors in which textiles, art, and antiques form a luscious and reflective setting. His design tells a story, bringing together a personal collection of art and furnishings gathered over the years during travels around the world.

A dramatic Venetian drapery in the foyer beckons to guests. In the living room, objects from a variety of periods blend together harmoniously. A baroque tapestry hangs adjacent to Harry Gates's modern canvas while leather and wrought-iron taborets contrast with Lucite tables nearby. A nineteenth-century Italian landscape in front of the window makes a visual pun, directing the eye to look outside for another tree-filled view. Pale hardwood floors lighten the interiors, while a sisal carpet keeps the room from feeling too formal.

Southern hospitality mixes with northern European grandeur in the oval dining room. Punctuating the Fortuny-inspired wall covering, vintage Tiffany porcelains alternate with a collection of hunting trophies, references to Sherrill's childhood in

Three mixed-media paintings by Brazilian artist Dudu Garcia hang above a Chesterfield sofa.
OVERLEAF: The flared arms of the sofa are a contemporary interpretation of the traditional Knole design.

the South. When not in use for dinner parties, the draped gateleg table holds a collection of interesting objects, arranged as curiosities.

The stately bedroom was partly inspired by childhood memories of George Vanderbilt's quarters at Biltmore in Sherrill's native North Carolina. In Sherrill's version, the centerpiece of the bed is a gilded Venetian overdoor with an ornate carving of the North Wind. Thick draperies, Fortuny pillows, and a castorino bedcovering add a luxurious softness. On both sides of the canopy, Dutch mirrors hang over contemporary paintings by a Franco-Mexican artist. Nearby, an eighteenth-century refectory table serves both as a desk and a display for treasured finds including a crystal orb, a nineteenth-century portrait, and a modernist bronze sculpture from Brazil. Blue-and-white ceramics from Mexico brighten the room with vivid colors and patterns.

Luxurious block-printed paper covers the dining room walls and complements the draped table.

Sherrill found the sixteenth-century armorial tapestry in the San Telmo district of Buenos Aires.

ABOVE: A nineteenth-century Dutch mirror with elaborate brass repoussé ornament adds grandeur to the living room. OPPOSITE: Spanish lithographs enliven the space above a Lucite table, where a collection of ceramic and glass vessels is displayed.

Chinese Fu dogs frolic next to a blue-and-white sugar bowl on the sideboard.

The table is set with an eclectic collection of Meissen dinnerware, Portuguese flatware, and Mexican silver accessories.

ABOVE: An arrangement of Tiffany plates with pierced rims interspersed with hunting trophies.
OPPOSITE: A tufted velvet window seat is installed at one end of the oval dining room. OVERLEAF: A richly carved
marble mantel, found in a Georgetown antique store, makes a strong architectural statement in the bedroom.

ABOVE: A carved Venetian overdoor serves as a headboard. OPPOSITE: An abstract painting by Washington artist Jacqui Crocetta hangs above the bedroom mantel.

An English refectory table
in the bedroom displays
a collection of treasures,
including a 1970s bronze
sculpture from Brazil.

Celebrating
Caribbean Culture

This inviting stucco villa at the Dorado Beach resort on the northern coast of Puerto Rico was designed as a weekend oasis where the clients and their guests can enjoy a vibrant collection of contemporary Puerto Rican artworks. The villa functions as both a private gallery and a setting for entertaining.

Sherrill and Solís, who had worked closely with the Colón-Nevares family on previous projects, sought to design a neutral architectural envelope with a restrained decor that would give the colorful paintings and sculptures center stage.

Marmorino plastered walls, travertine floors, and weathered wooden beams give the interior a rustic feel as do the oil-rubbed bronze finishes of the railings, door handles, and cabinet pulls. All of these elements blend together with the warm, earthy palette, the textured cotton and linen upholstery, raffia accents, and woven bamboo window shades. The overall sense of serenity and monastic calm brings forward the vivid colors and wild brush strokes of the paintings, strong reminders of the Caribbean culture that is celebrated at this house.

Large-scale canvases are focal points for the sitting areas in the double-height living room. A painting by Arnaldo Roche-Rabell faces Diógenes Ballester's energetic work across the room. The design also pays tribute to the clients' warm sense of

In the living room, Diógenes Ballester's expressive painting hangs
above a tailored sofa covered in chenille.

island hospitality. The long refectory table in the living room serves as a reception piece but transforms into a dining table for large gatherings. Two long raffia-covered benches can be pulled up to the table as seating for friends and family.

The festivities need not stay indoors. By extending the travertine flooring to the garden terrace, Sherrill and Solís created a spatial continuity between interior and exterior. They also reconfigured the front courtyard and back garden areas to easily accommodate tents for larger events. Drapes on the front entry and garage transform these spaces into cabanas. The lushly planted garden and fountains can be enjoyed from a chaise under a shaded pergola or from the patio dining area.

The gracefully reclining sculpture in the entry courtyard summarizes the essence of this weekend residence. *La Recostada* by Angel Botello welcomes guests, beckoning them to relax and enjoy the artful views.

Travertine in different colors defines the areas of the living space.

A muted palette is a foil to the vibrant colors of the art.
A playful work by José Morales hangs behind the refectory table.

ABOVE: Arnaldo Roche-Rabell's painting of bicycles inspired the circular seating
area and the selection of the curvilinear club chairs.
OPPOSITE: Ceramic works in the living room include a disk sculpture by
Jaime Suárez and a figurative sculpture by Toni Hambleton.

A painting by Epifanio Irizarry fits in well with the muted gray tones of the study.

A second-floor guestroom opens to a balcony overlooking the golf course.

A bronze sculpture of a rooster by Jorge Zeno sits bedside, but it is forbidden to crow early in the morning.

ABOVE: Rustic woven rush, cane and reed details are combined with linen fabrics to continue a casual feel of materials in this guestroom. OPPOSITE: In another guestroom, the organic shape of a driftwood lamp contrasts with the angularity of the handcrafted headboard.

PALACES OF VENICE

LEURS TABLES

ATLAS OF COLUMBUS AND THE GREAT DISCOVERI

COREN | The Intelligence o

Ode to Cambridge

Solís Betancourt was asked to open up the floor plan of this Washington cottage and fill it with soft, atmospheric colors and furnishings that were stylish and classical. In a way, the house tells a love story about its owners. The dining room mural is composed of scenes of Cambridge, Massachusetts, where the couple met, and sets the tone for the blues and hazy greens that make up the palette of the overall project.

Sherrill and Solís opted to join the living room and family room, which had previously been treated as two separate areas. Louis XVI-style sofas and mirrors in both sitting areas face one another and provide a spatial continuity. Painted strié wall treatments and silk carpets give these surfaces a subtle texture. The delicate forms of the gray-washed neoclassical-style furniture keep the rooms airy and light-hearted.

In the living room, four plush fauteuils surround an upholstered ottoman that functions as a coffee table. The fireplace wall is dressed up with paneling and a pair of gilt sconces. The arabesque motifs stenciled on the ceiling of the family room mimic the assortment of damask upholsteries and pillows. Recessed shelves and side tables provide book storage. An enclosed sunroom off the living area is a perfect place to settle with a book. The light-filled room opens onto a garden bordered with climbing roses and magnolias.

Subtle combinations of texture and color create a serene atmosphere in the family room.

A local artist was commissioned to transform the dining room into a misty depiction of historic Cambridge. Using the designers' fabric samples as a guide, he incorporated the luscious tones into the work. Neoclassical chairs surround an heirloom mahogany dining room table. Two serving tables were draped with fabric to help the room acoustically.

The kitchen and breakfast room act as the center of home life. Sturdy white cabinets and bleached wood floors give the room a fresh and tidy feel. A French wine-tasting table pulls up to a window banquette recessed between two storage cabinets. The family can sit here for meals or gather on the adjacent porch to take in the lush garden and softly gurgling fountain outside.

View from the dining room into the entry hall, with living room beyond. The soft palette is consistent throughout the house.

The living room and
family room are loosely
treated as mirror images
of one another, with a
soft division created by
the sheer linen portières.

A mural depicting Cambridge, Massachusetts, was commissioned to give the
dining room an atmospheric charm and serve as a memento for the owners.

A concealed doorway leads to the kitchen and breakfast area
where cabinetry defines a seating nook.

Custom-designed chaises provide comfortable seating in the garden room.

A simply dressed bed and a Queen Anne–style barrel wing chair create a comfortable setting in the master bedroom.

Contemporary Collaboration

This project represents a collaboration of great design minds. Landscape architect Richard Arentz, having purchased eighty acres of land in the Virginia countryside, invited architect Richard Williams and his friends and colleagues at Solís Betancourt to help him build a new residence. The house is carefully sited, perched on a ravine with mountain views in the distance. It is surrounded by different garden experiences, from carefully manicured areas to more untamed landscaping.

Sherrill and Solís wanted to create interiors that would reflect the owner's modernist aesthetic while still remaining full of warmth and personality. Working with Arentz, they ensured that the rooms have an appropriate scale and layout for entertaining and assembled a collection of bold artwork in keeping with the distinctive architecture of the house.

In the entry area, the cantilevered staircase, sculptural wooden spheres, and patterned carpet are a play in geometric forms. A massive stone wall, a visual continuation of the stone outside, divides the open floor plan.

The living room is surrounded on three sides by windows overlooking the lush foliage outside. An assortment of sofas and chairs was kept very low to give full access to the panoramic views. The clean lines of contemporary furniture contrast with a wooden slab coffee table, oriental carpet, and velvet upholstery, all of which add tactile richness. Antiques including a Chinese garden stool and a black and ivory scroll reflect the owner's admiration for Asian culture.

In the adjoining dining room, a glass wall sculpture by the New York–based artist Graham Caldwell provides a striking focal point. Its reddish brown hues are picked up

A drawing by artist Linn Meyers gives a burst of color to the neutral palette.

in the bronze frames of the Milo Baughman chairs and the wooden top of the custom-designed dining room table.

The contemporary aesthetic continues in a cooler palette in the kitchen and family room. The muted wood paneling gets a playful sparkle from an iridescent tiled backsplash in the kitchen. A variety of patterns, from the Chinese-style rug to the horn-veneered coffee table, enliven the sitting area.

A collection of cast stone heads mounted on the stair wall greets visitors going to the second floor. Here a series of intimate rooms are perfect for reading and relaxation. A massive bronze by Valerian Rybar dominates the sitting room, a persimmon cocoon that invites guests to unwind and enjoy the leisurely pace of country living.

Cantilevered oak stairs in the entry foyer give a sculptural presence.
OVERLEAF: Living room furniture was deliberately kept low to maintain the open, panoramic views.

ABOVE: Textured velvet upholstery complements the surface of the
Chinese drum table and the rough stone wall.
OPPOSITE: In the dining room, a glass sculpture by artist Graham
Caldwell sparkles and glows in the afternoon sun.

A pergola connecting
the main house to the
guest quarters is a
perfect spot for summer
buffets al fresco.

The second-floor landing is a gallery for works of art and an inviting area for reading.

The persimmon-colored walls of the second-floor sitting room add drama to the massive bronze sculpture by Valerian Rybar. OVERLEAF: In the family room, a horn-veneered coffee table sits on a boldly patterned rug.

ABOVE: The kitchen was designed to conceal many of its functional appliances and acts as a center for casual entertaining. OPPOSITE: The breakfast area overlooks the formal entry lawn and the forest beyond. OVERLEAF: In the guestroom the arrangement of pillows evokes an Asian aesthetic.

Historic Hues

Sited on land that was originally part of an eighteenth-century farm in Great Falls, Virginia, this house is deeply respectful of its past. The owners, who bought the house while it was still under construction, asked Solís Betancourt to develop colonial-inspired interiors that could house their collection of contemporary art.

From the entry hall, large openings lead to a series of spacious public rooms. The orange accents of the draped table and brocade upholstery help warm up the vastness of the space. Stately yet comfortable, the main living room is a lesson in symmetry and skillful layering of old and new elements. An eighteenth-century Irish wing chair seems right at home next to modern upholstered club chairs. A delicate glass cocktail table is a light counterpoint to the dark wood finishes of the period pieces. The golden and brown tones of the room get a jolt of intense blue from the Ed Ruscha work, which is flanked by a pair of Chinese vases. On the floor, an antique Tabriz carpet defines the main seating area. Tailored silk pleated curtains and roman shades visually heighten the windows and soften the architecture of the room.

Doorways on either side of the fireplace lead to the study, a room filled with books, antiques, and patterned upholsteries that convey a scholarly elegance. A federal painted bureau bookcase anchors the space between the windows. The bookshelves exhibit mementos that document the husband's academic career.

The owners brought the antique dining room furniture with them from their previous home. An immense sideboard, dubbed the "Queen Mary," fits comfortably into this spacious setting, and displays silver candelabras and serving pieces. To add

Draperies in the living room are mounted just below the crown molding to enhance the verticality of the space.

variety to the set of mahogany chairs, Sherrill and Solís included a pair of upholstered host and hostess chairs. Bring in a nearby tilt-top table, and these chairs become a perfect setting for an intimate fireside dinner for two. A damask runner on the table adds a layer of color, as does an arrangement of Imari porcelain pieces. A series of paintings, hunting trophies, and courting mirrors complete the colonial atmosphere.

The master bedroom is a serene space with large windows and pale flowing fabrics. The minimal palette and angular four-poster bed give it a modern sensibility, but detailed paneling, a brick fireplace, and pieces of period furniture keep the room true to the spirit of early America.

ABOVE: Traditional materials—clapboard, shingles, and fieldstone—are incorporated in the facade. OPPOSITE: The entry foyer demonstrates the designers' affinity for layering casual and refined textiles and materials.

Contemporary works of
art in the living room
inject color and contrast
with the collection of
traditional furnishings.

The artwork reads:

HELLO

I MUST BE GOING

An assortment of Asian porcelains give dashes of intense color and
pattern to the colonial-style dining room.

ABOVE: An office near the master bedroom displays a treasured painting that was a wedding present to the owners. OPPOSITE: A federal cabinet with delicate painted decoration integrates well with the otherwise masculine library.

Fortuny pleated draperies
are a contemporary
interpretation of
traditional bed hangings.

ABOVE: In the master bedroom, a vanity placed in a bay window gives a good view of the extensive grounds of the house. OPPOSITE: The fireside area in the master bedroom was designed as a comfortable spot for enjoying tea and coffee.

Mecox Monochrome

The gabled roof, walled courtyard, and softly rustling olive trees of this property are more strongly evocative of the spirit of southern France than that of the Hamptons. The owners wanted a vacation home that was quietly luxurious yet casual enough to withstand the sandy feet and wet bathing suits that are part of summertime family gatherings.

Solís Betancourt began by giving the 1960s house a much-needed update. The roofline was raised to give the central living area more height and make room for bedrooms upstairs. A vestibule was added to the entry area, and the courtyard was refreshed with stone paving and an antique fountain. The result is a residence with a European feel that also integrates into the local architecture of Water Mill, New York.

In the living room Sherrill and Solís removed all existing cased archways and bleached the red cedar beams to lighten the space. The supports were left exposed, accentuating the rustic farmhouse style. Wrought-iron brackets and stays were added to give the beams a more substantial presence. A large stone table anchors the two seating areas, and acts as an impromptu dining table when inclement weather keeps gatherings indoors. On axis with the stone fireplace, an intricate Italian mirror hovers gracefully on a linen backdrop.

The water views of Mecox Bay inspired the subdued interior palette, a mélange of muted grays and blues. To achieve this seemingly effortless layering of tones and the suggestion of dilapidated grandeur, Sherrill and Solís stained the terra-cotta floor tiles a light gray, covered the walls with coats of beige, violet, and gray-pigmented plaster, and chose tactile upholsteries and carpets rich in pattern but subtle in color. Paintings with soft colorations were placed in prominent axial locations. Antiques with an aged patina complete the dreamy, old-world atmosphere.

An architectural fragment creates a fanciful console table for the entry hall.
OVERLEAF: Solís Betancourt worked with architect
Brian Boyle to create a courtyard that has a European elegance.

In the kitchen, a nineteenth-century bookshelf with an old toile lining was converted into a hutch to store a collection of creamware. The kitchen cabinets were distressed and stained to match the weathered wood motif, with cut and tumbled mosaic stone tiles on the backsplash to complement the scuffed textures and tranquil color scheme.

Upstairs in the master bedroom, the opening to the curved staircase is ingeniously concealed by a hollowed-out teak cabinet. Two old window sashes, converted into closet doors, flank a window seat laden with Fortuny and crewel pillows. The bed floats in the middle of the room to provide full views of the water. In the master bathroom, two antique Turkish vessels act as stately sinks, set over a custom-designed storage cabinet.

The guesthouse is a quiet refuge. Guests can eat breakfast at the antique zinc-topped florist's table, or lounge on the bed, partially concealed behind a center-drawn linen curtain. Sunlight filtering into these rooms adds to their faded beauty and timeless elegance.

A massive stone table anchors the double-height living room.

A draped linen panel adds privacy to the sleeping
alcove in the guesthouse. Concrete pavers add texture
and accentuate the cottage feel of the space.

Painted iron garden chairs add a touch of whimsy to the tailored look of the daughter's suite.

In the master bedroom, casement window sashes were retrofitted as closet doors.

ABOVE: An antique Fortuny textile becomes a wall panel, framing a contemporary painting and unifying the master bedroom niche. OPPOSITE: The nineteenth-century French painting of a cow on a beach was selected as an allusion to Long Island's agrarian history.

The master bed is positioned in the middle of the room to allow unobstructed views of Mecox Bay.

Antique Turkish vessels are used as basins in the master bathroom.

ABOVE: The kitchen has hammered zinc countertops and rough-hewn open shelves, which provide easy access to a collection of creamware dishes. OPPOSITE: A found cupboard, lined with antique toile, is tucked in a niche in the breakfast area.

Portrait in Platinum

Just across the Hudson River from New York City, this stylish Englewood retreat seems a world away from the bustle of urban life. Defined by both the untamed forest of an adjacent nature preserve and its own manicured gardens, the residence feels like a hideaway. Solís Betancourt envisioned a house that was fresh and modern, with traditional references to harmonize with the neighborhood. The stucco walls, stone portico, and antique sconces give the facade a simplified classicism that blends with the contemporary feel of the interior. The designers worked closely with the landscape architect Barbara Paca to make sure that each room afforded expansive views of the green oasis outdoors.

A cool palette of silvery beige with the occasional hint of blue creates a look reminiscent of 1930s Hollywood glamour. In the kitchen and dining and living area, walnut floors add warmth to the color scheme as does the custom-designed dining room table. Contemporary Latin American black-and-white photographs add to the modern sensibility.

The room is sophisticated but practical. Sleek chrome dining room chairs are covered in a shimmering metallic fabric. Flowing draperies can be drawn to divide the space and create a more formal dining experience. The designers decided against upper cabinets in the kitchen to give the space a more airy feel and to take full advantage of the views.

The pyramid-vaulted ceiling gives the living room pavilion an added grandeur, as does a Murano glass chandelier. Chairs and sofas have clean, simple lines, while the wool and silk cheetah-inspired carpet gives the room a punch of pattern. A collection of Latin American paintings adds touches of bright color to the walls. In this room, like others in the house, the barrier between outdoor and indoor space is very fluid. The living room can also serve as a media room, where disguised speakers are wrapped in linen with nailhead details.

An allée of velvet draperies emphasizes the verticality of the spaces preceeding the living room entrance.

In the master bedroom, the pearlescent finish of the plaster walls, the silk curtains, and Lucite and glass accents give a reflective quality. The elegant bed consists of a silver-rubbed wood frame with a suede upholstered headboard and base. The plush pewter and silver carpet adds comfort and quiet.

The vistas from an adjoining master bathroom give it the feel of an enchanted tree house amid the canopy. The traditional paneling and marble floors receive a jolt of contemporary detail with the stainless-steel and glass sinks set in front of two large windows. Freestanding Venetian-style mirrors seem to hover gracefully in midair.

A small vestibule area leads into the private guest suite, where the soft beige palette contrasts with bold Cuban photographs.

The clients and their guests can gather in the outdoor loggia where flowing portières provide a shaded haven. This area includes comfortable sofas, a bar, and a television placed on axis with the steps to a waterfall pool. But the best diversion in this outdoor paradise are the streams and alleés of the terraced gardens.

Solís Betancourt collaborated with New York architect Ward Welch to create a classically inspired yet modern home. OVERLEAF: Expansive windows on three sides fill the living room with natural light.

The dining room and kitchen flow together for family use. For dinner parties, the draperies are closed and the effect is more formal.

ABOVE: A rosary is used decoratively, but it alludes to the Latin heritage of the owners. OPPOSITE: Black-and-white photographs by a Cuban artist create a bold geometry on the guestroom wall.

ABOVE: Cool metallic tones define the master bedroom and dressing room, evoking an art deco Hollywood glamour.
OPPOSITE: A desk area was created in the vestibule of the guestroom.

A parchment-covered desk serves both as a writing surface and as a bedside table.

An antique cabinet is flanked by contemporary glass basins on delicate stainless-steel bases.

Tropical Montage

Hidden amid the lush tropical foliage of San Juan's San Patricio neighborhood, this grand estate encapsulates a family's history and elegant style. The owners had renovated the structure in the 1970s when they first acquired the property, but the time had come to restore and rejuvenate the interior and exterior while simplifing the maintenance.

Solís Betancourt's goal was to design a lighter, fresher interior architecture while respecting the existing style that had become emblematic of the Colón-Nevares family's history and sense of tradition. This involved eliminating crown moldings and simplifying casings on the arched doorways. White lacquer furnishings give a unity and lightness to the renovated interiors. Extending the black and white marble floors throughout the house provided visual continuity. Simple forms upholstered in soft colors set off the gilt, cut crystal, and ornate wood carving of the antiques.

In the library, warm cocoa tones enhance the original millwork and create an intimate setting in which to admire Augusto Marín's painting. Ivory upholstery lightens the mood while referencing the principal palette of the house.

Olga Albizu's bold canvas *Yellow* hovers like a golden sun amid the Venetian plaster, lacquered furnishings, and crystal fixtures of the dining room. Nearby, Peter Fox's *Uniformal* provides an energetic burst of color to the adjacent gallery. Cuban artist Zilia Sanchez's sculptural canvas, hanging above one of two sofas in the living room, is a fine example of minimalist art.

The designers were careful to maintain elements of 1970s chic as well. A curved partition with heavy mirrored panels was translated into a dazzling wall of artist-made

Ormolu-mounted marble urns flank the archway to the living room.
OVERLEAF: Solís Betancourt sought the help of architect Evelio Pina for the recent renovation: Pina's father was the architect for the 1970s renovation.

mirror mosaics. The wall creates a dramatic setting for the staircase, with its black marble treads and brass rails. In the living room, a structural column covered in black mirrored glass was preserved as an axial connection to the bold black and white marble pattern in the entry area. Re-creating the moderne wooden grilles on the exterior windows in metal not only lightened their appearance, but also made them weather resistant. The same grilles were removed from railings on the upper balconies and replaced with glass to open up the garden views.

An essential component of the project was the design of an opulent master bedroom suite on the ground floor. The blue and green palette provides a meditative calmness while also referencing the pool and water gardens outside.

A custom mirror mosaic lines the curved wall of the dramatic circular staircase in the entry hall.
OVERLEAF: A sculptural canvas by Zilia Sanchez hangs in the living room.

The bold palette of a painting by Peter Fox is an electric presence
in the gallery adjacent to the dining room.

VOCES DE LA CULTURA

VISIONS of DESIGN   PANACHE

A modern
black-glass wall
crisply defines the
sculptural qualities
of the dining room
furniture and art.

ABOVE: The second-floor stair hall serves as a gallery for a rotating collection of paintings.
OPPOSITE: Augusto Marín's cubist-influenced painting brings together the geometric contemporary and ornate traditional furnishings in the library.

ABOVE: At the other end of the library, a tufted swivel chair and ormolu-mounted lacquer desk sit underneath a painting by Epifanio Irizarry. OPPOSITE: A bronze-doré sculpture of a Greek muse sits on the coffee table in the library.

THE COMPLETE COLLECTION OF
ANTIQUITIES
from the Cabinet of Sir William Hamilton

PIERRE-FRANÇOIS
HUGUES D'HANCARVILLE

TASCHEN

The collection of floral patterned china gives a cheerful
burst of color to the breakfast room.

In the master bedroom, a pair of chairs upholstered in silk embroidery gives a privileged
view of the cascading pool and gardens outside. OVERLEAF: The bed is set in an arched niche,
with a sophisticated play of curves in the headboard and mirror.

Light-weight furniture in the cabana allows the space to be easily
transformed for parties and dancing.

Park Avenue Polychrome

This prewar apartment in New York City represents a fresh take on the grandeur of Park Avenue style. The clients, Yaz and Valentín Hernández wanted an elegant setting for their collection of antiques and Latin American art with luxurious and welcoming spaces for entertaining. More simply put, they wanted the effect to be "fabulous."

Sherrill and Solís saw that the large rooms had great potential. The first step in the transformation was to imbue the space with lightness, achieved through a cream and gray stone floor in the entry and bleached hardwood floors in the rest of the apartment. The designers also wanted to pay homage to the building's history. The interior elevations throughout were enriched with traditional moldings to reflect its prewar origins. Existing structural beams were repeated to create a coffered ceiling that would incorporate the central air system and lighting.

From the entry, guests move into the grand public rooms. In the dining room, deep shades of orange, brown, and beige give a warmth to the majestic setting. The scale of the room becomes more intimate through the creation of a seating area at each end. Hidden closets serve a double function by breaking up the vast size of the space and also providing substantial storage for china and linens. A quilted niche is a dramatic setting for a poignant drawing by the Puerto Rican master Rafael Tufiño. The dilemma of an offset window is ingeniously solved by enlarging and centering the entablature casing and filling it with flowing silk draperies. The richness of the decor is tempered by the clean forms of the Lucite dining room table, mahogany side chairs, and Venetian-red silk upholstered armchairs. Crowning the interior is a crystal chandelier that hung in Yaz Hernández's childhood bedroom.

Bold contemporary forms are juxtaposed with traditional fabrics and paintings in the living room.

The designers took on a curatorial role by selecting and pairing appropriate works from the clients' large collection. The focal point of the living room is a painting of a guitar player by the Ecuadorean artist Oswaldo Guayasamín. The light shades of the silky carpet and velvet and chenille fabrics give a reflective sheen to the room and accentuate the warm and vibrant tones of the paintings installed by Sherrill and Solís. The rich browns of the antique wood furniture anchor the vibrant colors with the neutral textiles and upholstery.

The apartment has its private retreats as well. Murano glass lamps, celadon mohair club chairs, and silk draperies subtly embellish the master bedroom while Cornelius Baba's portrait of Yaz Hernández's mother adds a stately presence. The library is another small haven with its chocolate suede-lined shelves filled with books and fragments of ancient art.

Panel moldings and coffered ceilings were added to the space to create architectural interest.

Oswaldo Guayasamín's painting of a guitar player serenades guests in the living room. The sofa was designed by Solís Betancourt. OVERLEAF: The elaborate oriental carpet and handpainted silver-leaf wall covering of the dining room create an opulent environment for entertaining.

ABOVE: A sideboard holds a silver tea and coffee service and candelabra. OPPOSITE: A custom-designed entablature door casing frames a view to the entry foyer where Russian icons surround a mahogany secretary bookcase.

By adding closets in the master bedroom, the designers created a focal niche for the custom bed.

Riverside Still Life

Designed by renowned architect Fay Jones, this modernist home in McLean, Virginia, sits on a wooded ravine overlooking the Potomac River. A disciple of Frank Lloyd Wright, Jones was known for using native materials to integrate his buildings with the surrounding landscape. Soaring trees envelop the massive pillars, cast-concrete walls, and expansive windows that make up this prairie-style cathedral house. The owners commissioned Solís Betancourt to temper the strong architecture by creating warm and luxurious interiors that could house their large collection of religious art. The result is a striking juxtaposition between the baroque-inspired decor and the sleek, cantilevered structure.

To enter the house is to descend deep into the forest. A staircase near the driveway cascades downward, guiding visitors to a bridge-like walkway that leads to the front door. This area overlooks a spacious terrace with a fountain and swimming pool. Inside, an ancient statue of a river god is a fitting choice to greet guests. Recessed shelves on both sides of the hall display a rich collection of carved figures of saints, retablos, and art books. Mushroom, brown, and gold tones were used to enrich the interiors and complement the artwork.

The intimate entry hall leads to a series of spacious public rooms defined by high ceilings and ample skylights. In the living room, a colossal relief sculpture dominates the room, holding its own against the scale of the cast-concrete fireplace. The furniture is slightly rustic, with a Spanish colonial feel that blends well with the broad aesthetic traditions of the art. A custom-made chandelier illuminates the dining room in two ways: candles provide ambiance while the low-voltage lights help show off an

The suede-lined niche in the dining room displays European silver and decorative objects.

ever-changing still life of treasured objets arranged on the table below. Inside the suede-lined niche, a draped ledge and gilt mirror evoke the solemnity of an altar.

These public rooms spill out into a grand atrium with cathedral-height ceilings. Double-height draperies accentuate the verticality of the space and temper the austere windows and doorways. The ceiling beams were faux-painted to provide warmth and texture. On the upper level, the designers replaced a built-in banquette with a glass railing to keep the upstairs views open and unite the space with the lower level. In order to bring this sense of airiness and light into the kitchen, Sherrill and Solís inserted a skylight over the central island. Extending out into the foliage, the casual breakfast room has a tree-house feel.

The master bedroom may have a modern envelope, but its furnishings and paintings would feel appropriate inside a medieval castle. Sherrill and Solís designed a canopy that is both decorative and functional. The tailored fabric, held up by wrought-iron supports, helps shield the bed from early morning light that streams in from the skylight above. The supports are embellished with bronze Celtic motifs, a nod to the couple's Irish heritage. The plush carpet and sumptuous upholstery and pillows contribute to the hushed environment, a restful sanctuary nestled amid the trees.

A rustic entry door is the gateway into this quiet sanctuary.
OVERLEAF: A collection of religious sculpture from many periods and traditions is displayed on the bookcase.

On the left side of the entry, a partition wall separates the family room and living room. The wall also acts as a display for the owners' extensive collection of religious art and books. OVERLEAF: The bold artwork and furniture of the living room are appropriate for the large scale of the space.

Antique cut-velvet upholstery.

Needlepoint upholstery juxtaposed with a late-nineteenth-century Farahan Sarouk carpet.

ABOVE: A Spanish-colonial secretary serves as another display case for treasures. This sitting area off the living room is cantilevered to provide dramatic views of the Potomac River. OPPOSITE: A plank-top table in the dining room is a contemporary interpretation of a traditional refectory table. OVERLEAF: This seating area overlooks the living room below.

ABOVE: The breakfast room off the kitchen seems to float amid the treetops.
OPPOSITE: Sherrill and Solís designed a bronze armature bookcase to showcase an important carved stone relief.

Sherrill and Solís designed a regal canopy to shade the owners from the morning light. The cast-bronze supports are embellished with personalized Celtic motifs and semi-precious stones.

The linear design and massive cast-concrete construction are typical of Fay Jones's architecture. The owners chose him because of his respect for the natural environment.

A glimpse into a guestroom, perched above the Potomac River.

JOSÉ SOLÍS BETANCOURT, founder and president of Solís Betancourt Inc., has had a lifelong interest in art and architecture. Growing up in San Juan, Puerto Rico, he dedicated his spare time to drawing and painting, developing skills that would serve him well as an architecture student at Cornell University. He gained further experience at Skidmore, Owings & Merrill and at The Saladino Group, Inc.

PAUL MORGAN SHERRILL, a native of North Carolina, was greatly influenced by his grandparents who were painters and weavers and inspired him to study art and design. He graduated with honors from the University of North Carolina at Greensboro with degrees in human and environmental sciences and art. In 1992 Mr. Sherrill relocated to Washington, D. C. and began working as an interior designer for Solís Betancourt, Inc. Mr. Sherrill was named partner and serves as the vice president of the firm.

Acknowledgments

This book would not have been possible without the tremendous support and the patronage of our wonderful clients. They have provided us with the encouragement and inspiration to create this portfolio of very special work. Each project has been a journey in which we have grown and shared fond experiences. We would like to thank our clients for being such an integral part of the design process along the way.

Creating beautiful interiors is a collaboration that requires many talented artists, craftsmen, builders, furniture makers, installers, weavers, antique dealers, fabric houses, stonemasons, shippers, framers, painters, gilders, designers, and architects. We are so grateful to all of the skilled hands and hearts that have helped to support our vision.

We are so pleased to have this wonderful group of professionals interpreting our creative direction and bringing it into reality. The design process is most exciting when ideas are molded, embellished, and enhanced by other creative minds and the technical knowledge of their trade. We have enjoyed and are grateful for the many projects where we have worked closely with other design professionals, most notably Anthony Barnes, AIA, Barnes Vanze Architects; Richard Williams, AIA, Richard Williams Architects; Richard Arentz, SLA, Arentz Landscape Architects, LLC; Evelio Pina, AIA, Evelio Pina & Associates; Ward Welch, AIA, Coburn Architecture; Vilma Blanco and Sandy Balkow, OLA–Office of Landscape Architecture; Barbara Paca, Ph.D., Barbara Paca Landscape Preservation Planning; Holly Hunt, Holly Hunt, Ltd.; George Fritz, Horizon Builders; Jim Gibson, Gibson Builders; *Bill Cochran*, Accent General Contractors; Brian E. Boyle, AIA; Josef Gotsch, Innsbruck Renovations, LLC; Tim Rooney, All Around Technology.

Essential Elegance has been a dream of ours for many years. This aspiration was made possible by an extremely talented team of professionals. Our heartfelt thanks to Dana Demange, Marcos Galvany, Alfonso Sanchez, Doug Turshen, and Elizabeth White. We would also like to thank Paula Rice Jackson for introducing us to The Monacelli Press.

Finally, we thank our families for their steadfast support over the years.

Copyright © 2010 The Monacelli Press,
a division of Random House, Inc.

All rights reserved.

Published in the United States by
The Monacelli Press, a division of
Random House, New York.

The Monacelli Press and the M design
are registered trademarks of
Random House, Inc.

Library of Congress Control Number: 2010931300
ISBN 9781580932783

Designed by Doug Turshen and David Huang

Printed in China

www.monacellipress.com

10 9 8 7 6 5 4 3 2 1

Photographs by Marcos Galvany except as noted below:

Gordon Beal: 11–22
Karin Willis: 157–171
Jeff McNamara: 142–155
Walter Smalling Jr.: 41, 44–45, 52–53, 55, 57, 58–59